GW00985339

MEDITATIONS

ON THE
STATIONS OF THE CROSS

by
Cardinal John Henry Newman

All booklets are published thanks to the
generous support of the members of the
Catholic Truth Society

CATHOLIC TRUTH SOCIETY
PUBLISHERS TO THE HOLY SEE

CATHOLIC TRUTH SOCIETY
PUBLISHERS TO THE HOLY SEE

INTRODUCTION

Begin with an Act of Contrition

O my God,

because you are so good,

I am very sorry that I have

sinned against you

and by the help of your grace

I will not sin again.

The illustrations used in this edition are reproduced from
The Stations of the Cross at the Church of St Charles
Borromeo, Ogle Street, London, by kind permission of
the parish priest.

Photographs by Alan Suarez

THE FIRST STATION

Jesus is condemned to Death

V. We adore you, O Christ, and we bless you.
R. Because by your holy Cross you have redeemed the world.

Leaving the house of Caiaphas, and dragged before Pilate and Herod, mocked, beaten, and spit upon, His back torn with scourges, His head crowned with thorns, Jesus, who on the last day will judge the world, is Himself condemned by unjust judges to a death of ignominy and torture.

Jesus is condemned to death. His death-warrant is signed, and who signed it but I, when I committed my first mortal sins? My first mortal sins, when I fell away from the state of grace into which Thou didst place me by baptism; these it was that were Thy death-warrant, O Lord. The innocent suffered for the guilty. Those sins of mine were the voices which cried out, 'Let Him be crucified.' That willingness and delight of heart with which I committed them was the consent which Pilate gave to this clamourous multitude. And the hardness of heart which followed upon them, my disgust, my despair, my proud impatience, my obstinate resolve to sin on, the love of sin which took possession of me - what were these contrary and impetuous feelings but the blows and the blasphemies with which the fierce soldiers and the populace received Thee, thus carrying out the sentence which Pilate had pronounced?

Our Father, Hail Mary, Glory be to the Father.

V. Have mercy on us, O Lord.
R. Have mercy on us.

May the souls of the faithful, through the mercy of God, rest in peace. Amen.

THE SECOND STATION

Jesus receives His Cross

V. We adore you, O Christ, and we bless you.

R. Because by your holy Cross you have redeemed the world.

A strong, and therefore heavy, Cross, for it is strong enough to bear Him on it when He arrives at Calvary, is placed upon His torn shoulders. He receives it gently and meekly, nay, with gladness of heart, for it is to be the salvation of mankind.

True; but recollect, that heavy Cross is the weight of our sins. As it fell upon His neck and shoulders, it came down with a shock. Alas! what a sudden, heavy weight have I laid upon Thee, O Jesus! And though in the calm and clear foresight of Thy mind - for Thou seest all things - Thou wast fully prepared for it, yet Thy feeble frame tottered under it when it dropped down upon Thee. Ah! how great a misery is it that I have lifted up my hand against my God! How could I ever fancy He would forgive me unless He had Himself told us that He underwent His bitter Passion in order that he might forgive us. I acknowledge, O Jesus, in the anguish and agony of my heart, that my sins it was that struck Thee on the face, that bruised Thy sacred arms, that tore Thy flesh with iron rods, that nailed Thee to the Cross, and let Thee slowly die upon it.

Our Father, Hail Mary, Glory be to the Father.

V. Have mercy on us, O Lord.
R. Have mercy on us.

May the souls of the faithful, through the mercy of God, rest in peace. Amen.

THE THIRD STATION

Jesus falls the first time beneath the Cross

V. We adore you, O Christ, and we bless you.
R. Because by your holy Cross you have redeemed the world.

Jesus, bowed down under the weight and the length of the unwieldy Cross, which trailed after Him, slowly sets forth on His way, amid the mockeries and insults of the crowd. His agony in the Garden itself was sufficient to exhaust Him; but it was only the first of a multitude of sufferings. He sets off with His whole heart, but His limbs fail Him, and He falls. Yes, it is as I feared. Jesus, the strong and mighty Lord, has found for the moment our sins stronger than Himself. He falls, yet He bore the load for a while; He tottered, but He bore up and walked onwards. What, then, made Him give way? I say, I repeat, it is an intimation and a memory to thee, O my soul, of

thy falling back into mortal sin. I repented of the
sins of my youth, and went on well for a time; but at
length a new temptation came, when I was off my
guard, and I suddenly fell away. Then all my good
habits seemed to go at once; they were like a
garment which is stripped off, so quickly and utterly
did grace depart from me. And at that moment I
looked at my Lord, and lo! He had fallen down, and
I covered my face with my hands, and remained in a
state of great confusion.

Our Father, Hail Mary, Glory be to the Father.

V. Have mercy on us, O Lord.
R. Have mercy on us.

**May the souls of the faithful, through the
mercy of God, rest in peace. Amen.**

THE FOURTH STATION

Jesus meets His Mother

V. We adore you, O Christ, and we bless you.
R. Because by your holy Cross you have redeemed the world.

Jesus rises; though wounded by His fall, He journeys on, with His Cross still on His shoulders. He is bent down; but at one place, looking up, He sees His Mother. For an instant they just see each other, and He goes forward.

Mary would rather have had all His sufferings herself, could that have been, than not have known what they were by ceasing to be near Him. He, too, gained a refreshment, as from some soothing and grateful breath of air, to see her sad smile amid the sights and the noises which were about Him. She had known Him beautiful and glorious, with the freshness of divine innocence and peace upon His countenance; now she saw Him so changed and deformed that she could scarce have recognised Him, save for the piercing, thrilling peace-inspiring look He gave her. Still, He was now carrying the load of the world's sins, and, all-holy though He was, He carried the image of them on His very face. He looked like some outcast or outlaw who had frightful guilt upon Him. He had been made sin for us, who knew no sin; not a feature, not a limb, but spoke of guilt, of a curse, of punishment, of agony. Oh, what a meeting of Son and Mother! Yet there was a mutual comfort, for there was a mutual sympathy. Jesus and Mary - do they forget that Passiontide through all eternity?

Our Father, Hail Mary, Glory be to the Father.

V. Have mercy on us, O Lord.
R. Have mercy on us.

May the souls of the faithful, through the mercy of God, rest in peace. Amen.

THE FIFTH STATION

Simon of Cyrene helps Jesus to carry the Cross

V. We adore You, O Christ, and we bless You.

R. Because by Your holy Cross You have redeemed the world.

At length His strength fails utterly, and He is unable to proceed. The executioners stand perplexed. What are they to do? How is He to get to Calvary? Soon they see a stranger who seems strong and active - Simon of Cyrene. They seize on him, and compel him to carry the Cross with Jesus. The sight of the Sufferer pierces the man's heart. Oh, what a privilege! O happy soul, elect of God! He takes the part assigned to him with joy.

This came of Mary's intercession. He prayed not for Himself, except that He might drink the full chalice of suffering and do His Father's will; but she showed herself a mother by following Him with her prayers, since she could help Him in no other way. She then sent this stranger to help Him. It was she who led the soldiers to see that they might not be too fierce with Him. Sweet Mother, even do the like to us. Pray for us ever, Holy Mother of God, pray for us, whatever be our cross, as we pass along on our way. Pray for us, and we shall rise again though we have fallen. Pray for us when sorrow, anxiety, or sickness comes upon us. Pray for us when we are prostrate under the power of temptation, and send some faithful servant of thine to succour us. And in the world to come, if found worthy to expiate our sins in the fiery prison, send some good angel to give us a season of refreshment. Pray for us, Holy Mother of God.

Our Father, Hail Mary, Glory be to the Father.

V. Have mercy on us, O Lord.
R. Have mercy on us.

May the souls of the faithful, through the mercy of God, rest in peace. Amen.

THE SIXTH STATION

Jesus and Veronica

V. We adore You, O Christ, and we bless You.
R. Because by Your holy Cross You have redeemed the world.

As Jesus toils along up the hill, covered with the sweat of death, a woman makes her way through the crowd, and wipes His face with a napkin. In reward of her piety the cloth retains the impression of the Sacred Countenance upon it.

The relief which a mother's tenderness secured is not yet all she did. Her prayers sent Veronica as well as Simon - Simon to do a man's work, Veronica to do the part of a woman. The devout servant of Jesus did what she could. As Magdalen had poured the ointment at the feast, so Veronica now offered Him this napkin in His passion. 'Ah,' she said, 'would I could do more! Why have I not the strength of

Simon, to take part in the burden of the Cross? But men only can serve the Great High Priest, now that He is celebrating the solemn act of sacrifice.' O Jesus! let us one and all minister to Thee according to our places and powers. And as Thou didst accept from Thy followers refreshment in Thy hour of trial, so give to us the support of Thy grace when we are hard pressed by our foe. I feel I cannot bear up against temptation, weariness, despondency, and sin. I say to myself, what is the good of being religious? I shall fall, O my dear Saviour, I shall certainly fall, unless Thou dost renew for me my vigour like the eagle's, and breathe life into me by the soothing application and the touch of the holy Sacraments which Thou has appointed.

Our Father, Hail Mary, Glory be to the Father.

V. Have mercy on us, O Lord.
R. Have mercy on us.

May the souls of the faithful, through the mercy of God, rest in peace. Amen.

THE SEVENTH STATION

Jesus falls a second time

V. We adore you, O Christ, and we bless you.
R. Because by your holy Cross you have redeemed the world.

The pain of His wounds and the loss of blood increasing at every step of His way, again His limbs fail Him, and He falls on the ground.

What has He done to deserve all this? This is the reward received by the long-expected Messiah from the Chosen People, the Children of Israel. I know what to answer. He falls because I have fallen. I have fallen again. I know well that without Thy grace, O Lord, I could not stand; and I fancied that I had kept closely to Thy Sacraments; yet in spite of my going to Mass and to my duties, I am out of grace again. Why is it but because I have lost my devotional spirit, and have come to Thy holy ordinances in a cold, formal way, without inward affection. I became lukewarm, tepid. I thought the battle of life was over, and became secure. I had no lively faith, no sight of spiritual things. I came to church from habit, and because I thought others would observe it. I ought to be a new creature, I ought to live by faith, hope, and charity; but I thought more of this world than the world to come - and at last I forgot that I was a servant of God, and followed the broad way that leadeth to destruction, not the narrow way which leadeth to life. And thus I fell from Thee.

Our Father, Hail Mary, Glory be to the Father.

V. Have mercy on us, O Lord.
R. Have mercy on us.

May the souls of the faithful, through the mercy of God, rest in peace. Amen.

THE EIGHTH STATION

Jesus comforts the Women of Jerusalem

V. We adore you, O Christ, and we bless you.
R. Because by your holy Cross you have redeemed the world.

At the sight of the sufferings of Jesus the holy women are so pierced with grief that they cry out and bewail Him, careless what happens to them by so doing. Jesus, turning to them, said, 'Daughters of Jerusalem, weep not over Me, but weep for yourselves and for your children.'

Ah! can it be, O Lord, that I shall prove one of those sinful children for whom Thou biddest their mothers to weep? Weep not for Me,' He said, 'for I am the Lamb of God, and am making atonement at My own will for the sins of the world. I am suffering now, but I shall triumph; and, when I triumph, those souls for whom I am dying, will either be my dearest friends or my deadliest enemies. 'Is it possible? O my Lord, can I grasp the terrible thought that Thou really didst weep for me - weep for me, as Thou didst weep over Jerusalem? Is it possible that I am one of the reprobate? Possible that I shall lose by Thy passion and death, not gain by it? Oh, withdraw not from me. I am in a very bad way. I have so much evil in me. I have so little of an earnest, brave spirit to set against that evil. O Lord, what will become of me? It is so difficult for me to drive away the Evil Spirit from my heart. Thou alone canst effectually cast him out.

Our Father, Hail Mary, Glory be to the Father.

V. Have mercy on us, O Lord.
R. Have mercy on us.

May the souls of the faithful, through the mercy of God, rest in peace. Amen.

The Ninth Station

Again, a third time,
Jesus falls

V. We adore you, O Christ, and we bless you.

R. Because by your holy Cross you have redeemed the world.

Jesus had now reached almost to the top of Calvary; but, before He had gained the very spot where he was to be crucified, again He fell, and was again dragged up and goaded onwards by the brutal soldiery.

We are told in Holy Scripture of three falls of Satan, the Evil Spirit. The first was in the beginning; the second, when the Gospel and the Kingdom of Heaven were preached to the world; the third will be at the end of all things. The first is told us by St John the Evangelist. He says: 'There was a great battle in heaven. Michael and his angels fought with the dragon, and the dragon fought, and his angels. And they prevailed not, neither was their place found any more in heaven. And that great dragon was cast out, the old serpent, who is called the devil and Satan.' The second fall, at the time of the Gospel, is spoken of by our Lord when He says, 'I saw Satan, like lightning, falling from heaven.' And the third by the same St John: 'There came down fire from God out of heaven,... and the devil... was cast into the pool of fire and brimstone.' These three falls - the past, the present, and the future - the Evil Spirit had in mind when he moved Judas to betray our Lord. This was just his hour. Our Lord, when He was seized, said to His enemies, 'This is your hour and the power of darkness.' Satan knew his time was short, and thought he might use it to good effect. But - little dreaming that he would be acting in behalf of the world's redemption, which our Lord's passion and death were to work out - in revenge, and, as he thought, in triumph, he smote Him once, he smote Him twice, he smote Him thrice, each successive time a heavier blow. The weight of the Cross, the barbarity of the soldiers and the crowd, were but his instruments. O Jesus, the only-begotten Son of God, the Word Incarnate, we praise, adore, and love Thee for Thy ineffable condescension, even to allow Thyself thus for a time to fall into the hands and under the power of the Enemy of God and man, in order thereby to save us from being his servants and companions for eternity.

Or this

This is the worst fall of the three. His strength has for a while utterly failed Him, and it is some time before the barbarous soldiers can bring Him to. Ah! it was His anticipation of what was to happen to me. I get worse and worse. He sees the end from the beginning. He was thinking of me all the time He dragged Himself along, up the hill of Calvary. He saw that I should fall again in spite of all former warnings and former assistance. He saw that I should become secure and self-confident, and that my enemy would then assail me with some new temptation, to which I never thought I should be exposed. I thought my weakness lay all on one particular side which I knew. I had not a dream that I was not strong on the other. And so Satan came down on my unguarded side, and got the better of me from my self-trust and self-satisfaction. I was wanting in humility. I thought no harm would come on me; I thought I had outlived the danger of sinning; I thought it was an easy thing to get to heaven, and I was not watchful. It was my pride, and so I fell a third time.

Our Father, Hail Mary, Glory be to the Father.

V. Have mercy on us, O Lord.
R. Have mercy on us.

May the souls of the faithful, through the mercy of God, rest in peace. Amen.

THE TENTH STATION

Jesus is stripped, and drenched with gall

V. We adore you, O Christ, and we bless you.
R. Because by your holy Cross you have redeemed the world.

At length He has arrived at the place of sacrifice, and they begin to prepare Him for the Cross. His garments are torn from His bleeding body, and He, the Holy of Holies, stands exposed to the gaze of the coarse and scoffing multitude.

O Thou who in Thy Passion wast stripped of all Thy clothes, and held up to the curiosity and mockery of the rabble, strip me of myself here and now, that in the Last Day I come not to shame before men and angels. Thou didst endure the shame on Calvary, that I might be spared the shame at the Judgement. Thou hadst nothing to be ashamed of personally, and the shame which Thou didst feel was because Thou hadst taken on Thee man's nature. When they took from Thee Thy garments, those innocent limbs of Thine were but objects of humble and loving adoration to the highest Seraphim. They stood around in speechless awe, wondering at Thy beauty, and they trembled at Thy infinite self-abasement. But I, O Lord, how shall I appear if Thou shalt hold me up hereafter to be gazed upon, stripped of that robe of grace which is Thine, and seen in my own personal life and nature? O how hideous I am in myself, even in my best estate. Even when I am cleansed from my mortal sins, what disease and corruption is seen even in my venial sins. How shall I be fit for the society of angels, how for Thy presence, until Thou burnest this foul leprosy away in the fire of Purgatory?

Our Father, Hail Mary, Glory be to the Father.

V. Have mercy on us, O Lord.
R. Have mercy on us.

May the souls of the faithful, through the mercy of God, rest in peace. Amen.

Eleventh Station

Jesus is nailed to the Cross

V. We adore you, O Christ, and we bless you.

R. Because by your holy Cross you have redeemed the world.

The Cross is laid on the ground, and Jesus stretched upon it, and then, swaying heavily to and fro, it is, after much exertion, jerked into the hole ready to receive it. Or, as others think, it is set upright, and Jesus is raised up and fastened to it. As the savage executioners drive in the huge nails, He offers Himself to the Eternal Father as a ransom for the world. The blows are struck - the blood gushes forth.

Yes, they set up the Cross on high, and they placed a ladder against it, and, having stripped Him of His garments, made Him mount. With His hands feebly grasping its sides and cross-woods, and His feet slowly, uncertainly, with much effort, with many slips, mounting up, the soldiers propped Him on each side or He would have fallen. When He reached the projection where His sacred feet were to be, He turned round with sweet modesty and gentleness towards the fierce rabble, stretching out His arms, as if He would embrace them. Then He lovingly placed the backs of His hands close against the transverse beam, waiting for the executioners to come with their sharp nails and heavy hammers to dig into the palms of His hands, and to fasten them securely to the wood. There He hung, a perplexity to the multitude, a terror to evil spirits, the wonder, the awe, yet the joy, the adoration, of the holy angels.

Our Father, Hail Mary, Glory be to the Father.

V. Have mercy on us, O Lord.
R. Have mercy on us.

May the souls of the faithful, through the mercy of God, rest in peace. Amen.

THE TWELFTH STATION

Jesus dies upon the Cross

*V. We adore you, O Christ, and
we bless you.*
*R. Because by your holy Cross
you have redeemed the world.*

Jesus hung for three hours.
During this time He prayed for His
murderers, promised Paradise to the
penitent robber, and committed His Blessed Mother
to the guardianship of St John. Then all was finished,
and He bowed His head and gave up His Spirit.

The worst is over. The Holiest is dead and
departed. The most tender, the most affectionate, the
holiest of the sons of men is gone. Jesus is dead, and
with His death my sin shall die. I protest once for
all, before men and angels, that sin shall no more
have dominion over me. This Lent I make myself
God's own for ever. The salvation of my soul shall
be my first concern. With the aid of His grace I will

create in me a deep hatred and sorrow for my past sins. I will try hard to detest sin, as much as I have ever loved it. Into God's hands I put myself, not by halves, but unreservedly. I promise Thee, O Lord, with the help of Thy grace to keep out of the way of temptation, to avoid all occasions of sin, to turn at once from the voice of the Evil One, to be regular in my prayers, so to die to sin that Thou mayest not have died for me on the Cross in vain.

Our Father, Hail Mary, Glory be to the Father.

V. Have mercy on us, O Lord.
R. Have mercy on us.

May the souls of the faithful, through the mercy of God, rest in peace. Amen.

THE THIRTEENTH STATION

Jesus is taken from the Cross, and laid in Mary's bosom

V. We adore you, O Christ, and we bless you.
R. Because by your holy Cross you have redeemed the world.

The multitude have gone home; Calvary is left solitary and still, except that St John and the holy women are there. Then come Joseph of Arimathea and Nicodemus, and take down from the Cross the body of Jesus, and place it in the arms of Mary.

O Mary, at last thou hast possession of thy Son. Now, when His enemies can do no more, they leave Him in contempt to thee. As His unexpected friends perform their difficult work, thou lookest on with unspeakable thoughts. Thy heart is pierced with the sword of which Simeon spoke. O Mother most sorrowful; yet in thy sorrow there is a still greater joy. The joy in prospect nerved thee to stand by Him as He hung upon the Cross; much more now, without swooning, without trembling, thou dost receive Him to thy arms and on thy lap. Now thou art supremely happy as having Him, though He comes to thee not as He went from thee. He went from thy home, O Mother of God, in the strength and beauty of His manhood, and He comes back to thee dislocated, torn to pieces, mangled, dead. Yet, O Blessed Mary, thou art happier in the hour of woe than on the day of the marriage feast, for then He was leaving thee, and now in the future, as a risen Saviour, He will be separated from thee no more.

Our Father, Hail Mary, Glory be to the Father.

V. Have mercy on us, O Lord.
R. Have mercy on us.

May the souls of the faithful, through the mercy of God, rest in peace. Amen.

THE FOURTEENTH STATION

Jesus is laid in the Tomb

V. We adore you, O Christ, and we bless you.
R. Because by your holy Cross You have redeemed the world.

But for a short three days, for a day and a half - Mary then must give Him up. He is not yet risen. His friends and servants take Him from her, and place Him in an honourable tomb. They close it safely, till the hour comes for His resurrection.

Lie down and sleep in peace in the calm grave for a little while, dear Lord, and then wake up for an everlasting reign. We, like the faithful women, will watch around Thee, for all our treasure, all our life, is lodged with Thee. And, when our turn comes to die, grant, sweet Lord, that we may sleep calmly too, the sleep of the just. Let us sleep peacefully for the brief interval between death and the general resurrection. Guard us from the enemy, save us from the pit. Let our friends remember us and pray for us, O dear Lord. Let Masses be said for us, so that the pains of Purgatory, so much deserved by us and therefore so truly welcomed by us, may be over with little delay. Give us seasons of refreshment there; wrap us round with holy dreams and soothing contemplations, while we gather strength to ascend the heavens. And then let our faithful guardian angels help us up the glorious ladder, reaching from earth to heaven, which Jacob saw in vision. And when we reach the everlasting gates, let them open upon us with the music of angels; and let St Peter receive us, and our Lady, the glorious Queen of Saints, embrace us, and bring us to Thee, and to Thy Eternal Father, and to Thy Co-equal Spirit, Three Persons, One God, to reign with Them for ever and ever.

Our Father, Hail Mary, Glory be to the Father

Let us Pray: God who by the Precious Blood of Thy only-begotten Son didst sanctify the Standard of the Cross, grant, we beseech Thee, that we who rejoice in the glory of the same holy Cross may at all times and places rejoice in Thy protection through the same Christ, our Lord.

End with one Our Father, Hail Mary, and Glory be for the intention of the Holy Father.